Little Pebble™

Celebrate Winter

All About
Snowmen

by Kathryn Clay

CAPSTONE PRESS
a capstone imprint

Little Pebble is published by Capstone Press,
1710 Roe Crest Drive, North Mankato, Minnesota 56003
www.capstonepub.com

Library of Congress Cataloging-in-Publication information is on file
with the Library of Congress.
ISBN 978-1-4914-6007-8 (library binding)
ISBN 978-1-4914-6019-1 (paperback)
ISBN 978-1-4914-6031-3 (ebook PDF)

Editorial Credits

Erika L. Shores, editor; Cynthia Della-Rovere, designer;
Tracy Cummins, media researcher; Tori Abraham, production specialist

Photo Credits

Getty Images: Blend Images/Don Maso, 21; iStockphoto: FrankyDeMeyer,
19, Marilyn Nieves, 5, studio9400, 9; Shutterstock: Brykaylo Yuriy, 13,
KPG_Payless, 15, PRILL, 3, sellingpix, Design Element, Smit, cover,
Suzanne Tucker, 1, Vivid Pixels, 17, wizdata, 11; Thinkstock: Pavel
Losevsky, 7.

Printed in the United States of America in North Mankato, Minnesota.
032015   008823CGF15

Table of Contents

Winter Fun

Winter is here!

Snow is falling.

Let's build some snowmen.

Choose the right snow.

Dry snow won't stay together.

Sticky snow works best.

Build a Body

Make a body first.

Pack the snow

into a snowball.

Roll the ball along the ground.

Snow sticks to the snowball.

The ball gets larger.

Make another ball.

This is the snowman's middle.

Make a smaller ball.

This is the snowman's head.

The snowman needs arms.
Two sticks will work.

15

Funny Face

Time to add eyes
and buttons.
Matt uses rocks.

The snowman needs a nose.

Maddy uses a carrot.

All Dressed Up

Emma's snowman has a scarf.
She adds a purple hat.

How will you dress
your snowman?

Glossary

button—a round object used to fasten clothing

pack—to push together tightly

scarf—a length of fabric worn around the neck

snowball—a ball of packed snow

winter—one of the four seasons of the year; winter comes after fall and before spring

Read More

Aloian, Molly. *How Do We Know It Is Winter?*
Season Close-Up. New York: Crabtree Pub. Co., 2013.

Cox Cannons, Helen. *Snow.* Weather Wise.
Chicago: Heinemann, 2015.

Ghigna, Charles. *I See Winter.* North Mankato, Minn.:
Picture Window Books, 2012.

Internet Sites

FactHound offers a safe, fun way to find Internet sites related to this book. All of the sites on FactHound have been researched by our staff.

Here's all you do:
Visit *www.facthound.com*
Type in this code: 9781491460078

Super-cool stuff!

Check out projects, games and lots more at
www.capstonekids.com

Index